## The Whispering Lights

Flickers of brilliance in
Invite the wanderer, dr
Each twinkle tells of a tale untold,
Of worlds where mysteries gently unfold.

Guided by beams from a cosmic lore,
Footsteps lead to an unseen shore.
The pulse of the heavens, a beckoning call,
Whispers of wonder to one and to all.

## A Starlit Solace in Darkness

Under the blanket of velvety night,
Stars lend their glow, a comforting light.
In shadows we find a soft, sweet balm,
Starlit promises, a quiet calm.

Hearts take refuge in celestial glow,
Amidst the turmoil, our spirits grow.
Each spark above a flickering dream,
In darkness, we rise like a gentle stream.

Original title:
A Silent Star

Author: Sebastian Sarapuu
ISBN HARDBACK: 978-9916-79-861-4
ISBN PAPERBACK: 978-9916-79-862-1
ISBN EBOOK: 978-9916-79-863-8

# Silent Reveries in Galactic Tides

In stillness, dreams embrace the stars,
Whispers of time in shimmering bars.
Galaxies spin in twilight's grace,
Silent stories in boundless space.

Echoes of thoughts like softest sighs,
Drifting through cosmic, endless skies.
Tides of the universe ebb and flow,
In reveries where wonders glow.

## Shrouded Gleam of the Universe

Veils of mystery shroud the night,
Glimmers of knowledge, sparks of light.
In every shadow, secrets lie,
Waiting for souls who dare to fly.

Galactic dances in quiet grace,
A symphony played in vast, open space.
With every glance at the midnight scene,
We touch the cosmos, forever serene.

## The Still Beauty of Timelessness


In shadows deep, the moments freeze,
Whispers linger in the gentle breeze.
Time stands still, a quiet throne,
Where dreams are born, yet softly flown.

The stars above, like eyes are bright,
Guarding secrets of the night.
A canvas wide, of endless skies,
Where every heartbeat softly lies.

The river flows, a silent song,
Carrying tales of days gone long.
In stillness found, the heart may roam,
In timeless grace, we find our home.

## Illuminated Silence in the Abyss

In depths of dark, a light does gleam,
A whisper wrapped within a dream.
The silence stretches, thin as air,
Echoes dance with gentle flair.

Upon the edge of vast unknown,
Lies a truth that feels alone.
Stars ignite within the gloom,
Each one dancing, a heartbeat's tune.

The void embraces, calm and vast,
Holding futures, binding past.
In this quiet, courage brews,
As shadows bend and softly fuse.

## Secrets of the Night's Embrace

Moonlight spills on streets of stone,
Revealing whispers all alone.
Veils of night, so softly spun,
Guard the secrets of the sun.

In corners dark, where shadows play,
Mysteries linger, night and day.
Each whisper soft, a tale untold,
Wrapped in silver, blue, and gold.

Stars conspire with the breeze,
To tell of wishes, hearts at ease.
Underneath the velvet skies,
A world breathing, a heart's sigh.

# A Flicker in the Void

In spaces vast, where silence reigns,
A flicker glows, breaking chains.
Hope ignites, a spark anew,
Illuminating paths once few.

From shadows deep, a fire will rise,
Chasing the dark, filling the skies.
A heartbeat quick, a breath we share,
Lifting dreams from depths of despair.

This moment brief, yet rich with light,
Guides us forth through endless night.
In every flicker, flame, and spark,
Lives a story, bright in the dark.

# The Unheard Song of the Aurora

In the night sky, colors blend,
Whispers of light, they twist and bend.
Dancing softly, a silent song,
In frozen realms where dreams belong.

Beneath the shimmer, secrets dwell,
Echoes of stories, they never tell.
Each hue a note in nature's score,
Calling to hearts, forevermore.

As night unfolds, they weave their thread,
With every pulse, the darkness fed.
Auroras weave through ancient lore,
A symphony lost, forevermore.

In icy winds, the spirits sway,
Guiding travelers who've lost their way.
Through the vastness, they softly glance,
Inviting souls to join their dance.

Let us listen to the light's refrain,
In the silence, there's so much gain.
Tune our hearts to the cosmic song,
Feel the magic where we belong.

# Glistening in the Stillness

Upon the lake, the stars reflect,
Silent whispers, the night perfect.
Moonlight dances on water's skin,
A glistening world where dreams begin.

Gentle breezes brush by the trees,
Carrying tales in the evening breeze.
Crickets serenade the night anew,
Nature's chorus, a sound so true.

In the stillness, time stands still,
The heart finds peace, the mind can thrill.
With every breath, the beauty grows,
In this moment, the world bestows.

Ripples form in soft embrace,
Mirroring dreams, a tranquil space.
Under the sky, lost in the night,
We find solace in nature's light.

Let us linger where shadows play,
In glistening moments that fade away.
For in stillness, our souls can soar,
Finding treasures forevermore.

# A Cosmic Canvas of Silent Light

Stars like paint on canvassed night,
Brushing the sky with soft delight.
Each spark a story, a secret shared,
In the vastness, no heart is spared.

Galaxies swirl in a cosmic dance,
Inviting us to take a chance.
Silent wonders lie in the dark,
Each twinkle ignites a hopeful spark.

Nebulae bloom with colors bright,
Chasing shadows, embracing the light.
Infinite realms stretch wide and free,
A symphony of galaxies.

Through telescope eyes, we journey far,
Mapping our dreams among each star.
Every twinkle, a dream in flight,
Painting hopes on this canvas of light.

In the silence, connections grow,
We find our place in the cosmic flow.
Together we gaze at the stellar sea,
Finding joy in this vast mystery.

# The Sigh of Celestial Bodies

In the midnight, the planets sigh,
Whispers of time, drifting by.
Their gentle rhythms guide us home,
In stellar isolation, we roam.

Each orbit tells a tale of fate,
Woven in silence, we contemplate.
Comets trail with a fleeting kiss,
Marking moments we might miss.

Galaxies spin in a cosmic dream,
Carving out paths in a starlit stream.
With every sigh, a memory flows,
A universe boundless, where love grows.

Across the void, we seek the light,
Filling the darkness with hope so bright.
Celestial bodies remind us why,
To cherish the stars that hear our cry.

So let us breathe in this mystic air,
With every heartbeat, we're drawn to dare.
For in the sighs of the universe vast,
We find our present, our future, our past.

# Hidden Illuminations in the Calm

In the hush of twilight's glow,
Whispers dance on breezes slow.
Stars awaken, softly sigh,
Secrets hidden, not yet nigh.

Moonlight paints the quiet ground,
Dreams and shadows twirl around.
Hearts lay bare, in stillness found,
Hope and solace, all around.

Gentle ripples touch the shore,
Echoes calling, evermore.
Life's reflections, calm and clear,
In the silence, we draw near.

Nature's breath, a tender sigh,
Underneath a painted sky.
Hidden gems in silent streams,
Hold the weight of whispered dreams.

Stillness deepens, time stands still,
Mind and spirit, bend to will.
In the quiet, truth appears,
Guiding light through all our fears.

# Reflections of Forgotten Epiphanies

In the mirror of the past,
Moments fleeting, shadows cast.
Thoughts like ripples form and fade,
Carrying wisdom, the heart's crusade.

Starlit paths we used to roam,
Voices soft, a distant home.
Journey etched in faded lines,
Fragments dance where memory shines.

Time's embrace holds lessons dear,
Epiphanies whisper near.
Lost in echoes, we retreat,
Searching for the pulse of beat.

In the stillness, answers flow,
Revelations, a gentle glow.
Bringing forth the light of day,
Guiding souls along the way.

Shattered dreams find strength to rise,
Reflections caught in painted skies.
Through the past, we forge ahead,
Carrying hope for paths widespread.

## Tranquil Radiance of Unexplored Skies

Above the trees where silence reigns,
Clouds drift softly, free of chains.
Colors blend in twilight's art,
Awakening the wandering heart.

In the expanse where dreams take flight,
Starlit visions grace the night.
Whispers linger on the breeze,
Carried forth with gentle ease.

Moonbeam trails across the field,
In their light, our souls are healed.
Every glance at distant stars,
Holds the promise of who we are.

Beneath this vast and tranquil dome,
Every wish finds strength to roam.
In uncharted realms we see,
Radiance born of hopes set free.

So let us wander, hand in hand,
Across the skies, through every land.
In the quiet, we will find,
The luminous spark that frees the mind.

## Captured in Celestial Muteness

Stars whisper softly in the night,
Silent tales of ancient light.
Waves of time in stillness flow,
Wrapped in dreams we do not know.

The moon casts shadows on the ground,
In this peace, no echoes sound.
Hearts entwined in tranquil grace,
Lost forever in this space.

Gaze upwards where the blackbirds soar,
In their flight, the silence roars.
Captured moments held so dear,
Radiate through calm and fear.

With every heartbeat, silence sings,
A symphony of hidden things.
In the stillness, secrets dwell,
In the quiet, we're compelled.

In celestial halls, time stands still,
Breathless wonders weave and thrill.
Under the fabric of the night,
Captured dreams take gentle flight.

# The Enigmatic Glow of Nightfall

A shroud descends, the colours fade,
In twilight's grasp, the world is laid.
Echoes whisper through the trees,
Nightfall dances on the breeze.

Stars ignite in velvet skies,
Their golden light a sweet surprise.
Mysteries wrapped in folds of dark,
Where every shadow leaves a mark.

The world slows down; we pause to breathe,
In every corner, spirits weave.
A glow emerges, soft and bright,
In the silence of the night.

Old stories linger, softly told,
As night enfolds, a blanket gold.
Moonlit whispers kiss the air,
In the quiet, we share our care.

In the heart of dark, we find our way,
Guided by the stars' ballet.
The enigmatic glow will last,
Carrying forward from the past.

# Echoes of the Invisible

Thoughts collide in silent streams,
Unseen realms of distant dreams.
Voices linger, yet unheard,
In the stillness, all deferred.

The heartbeats blend with fading light,
Whispers of the starry night.
In between the breaths we take,
Lies the magic we create.

Invisible threads connect us all,
A tapestry, unseen yet tall.
Moments woven, time aligned,
In the spaces, love confined.

Soft shadows dance on empty walls,
A symphony that gently calls.
Echoes ripple through the air,
Invisible, but always there.

In the silence, truths emerge,
Quiet forces start to surge.
We listen close, the world unfolds,
Echoes rich with tales untold.

## Under the Veil of Cosmic Serenity


Beneath the stars, a world at peace,
Where every worry finds release.
The cosmos hums a gentle tune,
Wrapped within the light of moon.

Galaxies spin in endless grace,
Creating soft, enchanted space.
The nightingale sings sweetly clear,
In the serenity, we draw near.

Time dissolves in the quiet night,
Endless moments, pure delight.
Within this veil, our spirits soar,
Longing for just a little more.

Dreams unfurl beneath the sky,
As constellations wink and sigh.
Each twinkling star, a distant friend,
Under this spell, we suspend.

In cosmic arms, we intertwine,
With every heartbeat, love defines.
Under the veil, we seek and find,
A sanctuary in the mind.

# Veiled in Cosmic Tranquility

Stars whisper secrets to the night,
Moonlight dances, soft and bright.
Galaxies swirl in silent grace,
Time pauses in this vast, warm space.

Clouds cradle dreams like gentle streams,
Wishes carried on starlit beams.
The universe hums a lullaby,
As the cosmos breathes a sleepy sigh.

Vast horizons in dark embrace,
Infinite wonders, a sacred place.
Eternal stillness wraps the soul,
In the silence, we become whole.

Each twinkle holds a timeless tale,
In the quiet, hope will prevail.
Veiled in the calm of endless night,
We find solace in the cosmic light.

Beneath the sky's celestial dome,
The heart finds peace, the spirit home.
Veiled in tranquility ever true,
Infinity sings, we feel anew.

# The Framework of Stillness

Silence cradles the twilight hour,
Whispers linger, soft as a flower.
Time stands still, a patient friend,
In the calm, our thoughts suspend.

Misty veils cover the dawn's light,
Moments frozen in pure delight.
The canvas waits, serene and bare,
In each heartbeat, stillness we share.

Waves of calm wash over the mind,
In this space, true peace we find.
Breath by breath, we gently weave,
Threads of quiet in which we believe.

Stars emerge in the velvet sky,
Framed in stillness, dreams can fly.
Each flicker speaks of tales untold,
In the void, a silence bold.

The framework holds our fleeting thoughts,
Nestled in layers, wisdoms sought.
In stillness we grasp the grand design,
With each pause, the soul aligns.

## Soft Echoes of the Universe

Tides of stardust flow through space,
In their echoes, we find a trace.
Whispers of ages, soft and clear,
Carried on winds that draw us near.

Galaxies spin with gentle grace,
Holding mysteries we long to face.
In the vastness, our hearts unite,
Listening deeply to the night.

Comets streak in a silent dance,
Each a moment, a fleeting chance.
Echoes ripple through time and space,
Reminding us of our sacred place.

In the quiet, voices intertwine,
Threads of existence, a sacred line.
Soft echoes carry the light we seek,
In the stillness, our spirits speak.

All around, the cosmos sighs,
A gentle breath in endless skies.
With every pulse, the universe flows,
In soft echoes, our essence grows.

## The Softest Brightness

Morning blooms with a tender hue,
Softest brightness, a world anew.
Golden rays gently kiss the ground,
In this warmth, our joys abound.

Petals open to the sun's embrace,
Nature's canvas, a sacred space.
Shadows fade in the light's warm glow,
In soft brightness, our spirits flow.

Each whispering breeze tells a tale,
Of love and hope that shall not pale.
A quiet moment where dreams ignite,
In the softest brightness, hearts take flight.

Color cascades in a gentle stream,
Awakening visions, igniting dreams.
In this radiance, fears dissipate,
As we bask in the light of fate.

With every dawn, a promise reigns,
In the softest brightness, joy sustains.
Together we rise, hand in hand,
In a world painted by love, we stand.

# The Starlit Soliloquy

Beneath the sky, the stars engage,
A dance of light, on night's grand stage.
Whispers echo in the gentle breeze,
Thoughts drift softly, like autumn leaves.

Each twinkle tells a tale untold,
Of dreams and wishes, brave and bold.
Silence cradles the secrets we keep,
In the heart of night, where shadows creep.

Moments linger, then fade away,
As dawn approaches, brightening gray.
Yet in this peace, we find our way,
Through starlit paths, we gently sway.

The cosmos sings, a melody rare,
In the stillness, we become aware.
Of love and loss in the vast expanse,
Beneath the stars, we take our chance.

So here we sit, just you and I,
In this quiet, where dreams can fly.
A starlit soiree, no need to speak,
For in this moment, we both feel weak.

## Transcendent Silence of the Night

In the dark, a stillness reigns,
Where whispers float like gentle trains.
Stars align in perfect peace,
Wrapping hearts in sweet release.

Moonlit shadows dance and sway,
Painting dreams in shades of gray.
Nature stirs, a soft embrace,
In the night's transcendent grace.

The world slows down, time stands still,
A sacred pause, a tranquil thrill.
Silence deepens like the sea,
Filling spaces endlessly.

As constellations gently spin,
We find where all our thoughts begin.
In every glance, a story told,
In the quiet, we are bold.

With every breath, the night is whole,
A canvas vast, it holds our soul.
Together here, we paint our night,
In transcendent silence, pure delight.

## Veiled Brilliance in the Ether

Hidden lights in velvet skies,
Glisten softly, with wary eyes.
Whispers of the universe flow,
In veiled brilliance, secrets grow.

The moon, a guardian up high,
Sheds its glow on dreams that fly.
Stars, like thoughts, in clusters cling,
In this space, our hopes take wing.

Echoes weave through time and space,
Painting night in a tender grace.
Every heartbeat, a silent prayer,
In the ether, we find care.

Translucent visions drift and sway,
Guiding us on this starry way.
With every shimmer, we are bound,
In veiled brilliance, love is found.

So let us wander, hand in hand,
Through this cosmic, sacred land.
For in the dark, we'll weave our dreams,
In the night's soft, glowing beams.

## Soft Gleams of the Cosmic Whisper

Gentle glimmers in the night,
Softly cradle hopes in flight.
Celestial songs drift from afar,
Echoing dreams wrapped in a star.

Floating whispers through the air,
Fading worries, light as hair.
In the silence, hearts align,
With the cosmos, pure and divine.

The world dissolves, just you and me,
In this moment, we are free.
Embers flicker, softly glow,
Guiding paths we yearn to know.

Beneath the arch of endless night,
Soft gleams flow, a sweet delight.
In every glance, love's subtle trace,
In cosmic whispers, we find grace.

So take my hand, let's drift away,
In the starlit dreams where shadows play.
With every sigh, the universe sings,
In soft gleams, the heart takes wings.

# Glimmers in the Absence of Sound

In a silent room, shadows play,
Whispers of night, drift away.
Stars glisten on the velvet sky,
Echoes of dreams, softly sigh.

Moonbeams dance on the still glass,
Time creeps by, yet moments last.
Fleeting glimmers, bright and rare,
In the stillness, magic's there.

Thoughts weave gently through the air,
In every corner, secrets stare.
The hum of life, a distant hum,
In absence, feelings quietly come.

Heartbeats thrum in hidden beats,
Between the silence, life retreats.
A world unknown, yet so profound,
Glimmers emerge in the soft sound.

Beneath the hush, the truth we find,
In the shadows, peace entwined.
Glimmers shine where silence reigns,
In the absence, joy remains.

# The Space Between Heartbeats

In each pause, a whisper waits,
Time unfolds, it hesitates.
The heartbeat's dance, a sacred art,
Moments held, a fragile start.

Echoes linger in the air,
Suspended breath, a gentle prayer.
In that space, the soul can feel,
Emotions deep, a silent reel.

A heartbeat's glow, a tender light,
Illuminates the edge of night.
Between the thumps, the world expands,
In quiet rhythms, life commands.

Dreams take flight in tranquil beats,
Where longing and the stillness meets.
The space, a canvas, vast and wide,
In silence, truth and hope abide.

Count each pause, a quiet sound,
In each moment, love is found.
The heartbeat's echo sings so true,
In space between, I'm drawn to you.

# Radiant Quietude of Infinity

In the vastness, silence reigns,
Stars whisper tales of old campaigns.
Galaxies swirl in gentle grace,
Time flows softly in endless space.

Nebulas bloom like flowers bright,
Colors twinkle in the night.
Radiance swells from deep within,
A quietude that draws us in.

Infinity holds its breath so still,
Moments stretch, bend to will.
Interstellar dreams weave and spin,
In this tapestry, we begin.

Peace unfolds like morning light,
In the dark, warmth finds its flight.
Every heartbeat echoes far,
In the void, we find who we are.

With each gaze, a journey made,
In the quiet, fears do fade.
Radiant whispers, stars align,
In the stillness, we define.

# Dreams Unseen in the Starlight

In the twilight, shadows grow,
Portals open, visions flow.
Dreams unfold in softest shades,
Unseen wonders, serenades.

Beneath the glow of silver beams,
Whispers linger, woven dreams.
The fabric rich, with stories spun,
In starlight's clutch, we become one.

Echoes of hopes, they softly tread,
On the surface of what's unsaid.
Chasing night's elusive sighs,
In dreams unseen, the spirit flies.

The universe unfolds its hand,
Crafting secrets, so unplanned.
In starlit paths, we find our way,
To worlds where night turns into day.

A dance of thoughts, a soft revive,
In each dream, we feel alive.
Unseen beauty fills the night,
In starlight's glow, our hearts take flight.

# Serenity in Starlight

Under the vast, shimmering sky,
Whispers of night softly sigh.
Gentle dreams weave and play,
In the embrace of twilight's sway.

Silence drapes the earth in peace,
As time slows, worries cease.
Stars above begin to gleam,
Crafting hope in a quiet dream.

Moonlight dances on the ground,
In this sacred space, joy is found.
A canvas of wonders so bright,
Guiding souls through gentle night.

Beneath each twinkling star's glow,
Hearts connected, spirits flow.
Moments linger, slow and wide,
In the beauty where we confide.

Embracing the calm, we abide,
In starlit wonder, side by side.
Here in silence, we will stay,
Forever lost in night's ballet.

## The Hushed Radiance

Softly glimmering in the dark,
The moon ignites a tender spark.
Glistening dreams, a gentle embrace,
Whispers of love weave through space.

Shadows dance in silver light,
Painting secrets of the night.
Time surrenders, stands still,
In this realm where hearts can thrill.

The world fades into a sigh,
As constellations drift on high.
Breaths unite in peaceful tones,
In starlit calm, we find our home.

A warmth that carries through the air,
In this haven, free of care.
Every heartbeat finds its tune,
In the glow of a silent moon.

In this sacred, quiet place,
We discover love's true grace.
With every star, we will abide,
In the hush where dreams reside.

## Celestial Solitude

In the stillness of the night,
Hearts embrace the soothing light.
Gazing up at the endless sky,
Where whispered wishes softly lie.

A canvas stretched with glimmering stars,
A universe that heals our scars.
In solitude, the spirit sings,
Finding solace in gentle wings.

Voices of the night unfold,
Stories of each dream retold.
Time passes with a tender hand,
Guiding us to a distant land.

Twilight wraps us in its song,
Where we feel forever strong.
In celestial grace, we mend,
Learning how the heart can bend.

Every twinkle, every beam,
Invites us deeper into the dream.
In quietude, our souls align,
In celestial solitude, we shine.

## Invisible Serenade

A melody drifts on the breeze,
Carried gently through the trees.
The night whispers secrets untold,
In hues of silver and gold.

Hearts awaken, a soft refrain,
In the quiet, there's no pain.
Each note dances, fluttering light,
Guiding us through the woven night.

Stars begin their thrilling song,
Echoing where we belong.
Voices blend in perfect tune,
Under the watchful, caring moon.

Threads of magic weave and flow,
Bringing warmth to the night's glow.
In every heartbeat, love draws near,
In this serenade, crystal clear.

Invisible tunes softly play,
Illuminating our path each day.
In the hush, our spirits rise,
Embraced forever by the skies.

# Secrets Among the Constellations

Whispers dance in the night sky,
Stars hold tales yet to be told.
In their glow, dreams softly sigh,
Paths of fate in silver unfold.

Celestial maps drawn with grace,
Wonders wrapped in cosmic light.
Every twinkle, a secret place,
Guiding wanderers through the night.

Nebulas cradle the unknown,
Veils of mystery cloak the years.
In the quiet, the heart has grown,
Counting joys, and tracing fears.

Galaxies swirl in endless dance,
Infinite stories blend and weave.
Hope ignites in each fleeting glance,
In starlit paths, we dare believe.

Connect the dots of fate and time,
In each spark, an echo sings.
In the vastness, we dare to climb,
Living the dreams that starlight brings.

## The Stillness Beneath the Light

Calm descends on the shadowed ground,
A hush that cradles weary hearts.
In the silence, wisdom is found,
Soft as dusk as the day departs.

Trees whisper to the night's embrace,
Leaves rustle like a gentle sigh.
Moonlight paints a serene face,
As stars awaken in the sky.

Time seems to still, a breath held tight,
Each moment lingers, sweet and rare.
In the quiet, souls take flight,
Yearning hearts find solace there.

The world fades to a distant hum,
Each heartbeat marks the endless flow.
In stillness, life's melodies come,
Filling voids that we long to know.

Embrace the peace, let spirits soar,
Where light and shadows intertwine.
In stillness, we forever explore,
The beauty of knowing we are divine.

# Luminous Shadows in the Dark

Beneath the veil of nightly dreams,
Shadows flicker, dance, and play.
In their depths, a glow redeems,
Illuminating every stray.

Stars weave tales in dark's embrace,
Guiding lost souls through despair.
Each flicker shines with grace,
A promise whispered in the air.

Light shades creep through twilight's glow,
Secrets hidden, truths revealed.
In the dark where wishes flow,
Hope emerges, gently healed.

The moon, a guardian in flight,
Casting dreams upon the ground.
In shadows, find the heart of light,
Where all the lost are truly found.

Luminous paths in quiet surround,
Guiding hearts through fears and doubt.
In shadows deep, love's pulse resound,
We find the light, we leap, we shout.

# Murmurs from the Galactic Abyss

Deep in the cosmos, whispers twine,
A symphony of ancient songs.
Faint echoes from the stars align,
Carrying tales where time belongs.

In the void, shadows softly speak,
Their secrets woven through the night.
Each murmur, a connection deep,
A call to wander, to seek the light.

Galaxies swirl, a cosmic dance,
Creating patterns in silence vast.
In each twinkle, there's a chance,
To touch the past and hold it fast.

Waves of starlight linger near,
Guiding dreams across the way.
In their warmth, we conquer fear,
Finding hope in the Milky Way.

Through infinity, journeys unfold,
The abyss reveals its tender flair.
In the murmurs, mysteries told,
A universe we long to share.

# Whispers of Celestial Glow

In twilight's tender hand, they sway,
The stars begin their gentle play.
Soft whispers dance through night's embrace,
While dreams alight in cosmic grace.

The silver moon, a watchful eye,
Keeps secrets held in darkened sky.
Each flickering light, a story told,
Of ancient paths and futures bold.

Awake, the night sings lullabies,
As constellations fill our skies.
A tapestry of fate unspooled,
In silence shared, our hearts are ruled.

The gentle breeze, it hums along,
A symphony both soft and strong.
With every pulse, the cosmos flows,
In whispered love, the essence grows.

So linger here beneath the glow,
Where time suspends, and dreams can flow.
In night's dear arms, we find our peace,
And with each heartbeat, joys increase.

# Veil of Cosmic Stillness

Beneath the sky, the silence weaves,
A tapestry that softens leaves.
Stars twinkling in the deep abyss,
Invite the soul to find its bliss.

As shadows lengthen, peace descends,
The universe its heart extends.
Each moment holds a timeworn grace,
Where whispers linger, life's embrace.

A gentle hush surrounds our flight,
In cosmic dreams that fill the night.
With every breath, the stillness grows,
In hallowed calm, our spirit knows.

The heavens gleam in quiet tones,
Reminding us of ancient phones.
In clarity, we find our way,
Through mystic paths where starlights play.

So let us wander, hand in hand,
Within the vast and dusky land.
In stillness wrapped, we find our trust,
Where cosmic souls embrace the dust.

# The Quiet Luminance

In shadows cast by day's farewell,
A quiet light begins to swell.
Luminance that softly glows,
Guiding hearts, where chance bestows.

With every spark, a story shines,
Of distant worlds and tangled lines.
Each flicker speaks of paths once crossed,
In luminal threads, we find the lost.

The night unveils a tapestry,
Of dreams encoded, wild and free.
A murmured urge to seek, explore,
To chase the light through every door.

So pause a while, and breathe it in,
Let quiet be where we begin.
For in this glow, our truths align,
In twilight's arms, our souls entwine.

Through gentle rays, we feel alive,
In luminous moments, hopes revive.
Together forged in peaceful dance,
In quiet light, we take our chance.

# Echoes of Night's Embrace

In depths of night, a whisper flows,
Through starlit skies where silence grows.
Echoes linger, soft and low,
In shadows deep, their secrets glow.

The moon, a gentle guardian bright,
Illuminates the hidden plight.
With silver beams, it shares its song,
Of time and place where we belong.

Among the trees, a rustling sound,
The heartbeat of the night, profound.
Nature breathes in rhythmic sway,
While dreams take flight and lose their way.

The cosmos sways with tender grace,
In every pulse, a warm embrace.
As echoes dance on midnight's breath,
We find our peace beyond the death.

So let the night enfold our fears,
In starlit waves that dry our tears.
With hope reborn, we shall explore,
The echoes of what came before.

# When Light Knows No Sound

In the dawn where silence reigns,
Golden beams break gently free,
Whispers of the waking plains,
Nature's breath, a symphony.

Colors dance without a sound,
Each hue tells a secret tale,
In this peace, no voices found,
Harmony begins to sail.

Shadows shift and softly play,
While time flows like a gentle stream,
In the light of breaking day,
Reality blends with a dream.

Moments linger, fleeting fast,
Underneath the azure skies,
Here the echoes of the past,
Merge with whispers and soft sighs.

When the light greets day anew,
In a world where stillness stays,
Listen closely, feel it too,
As the dawn begins to blaze.

# The Tranquil Glow Above

Stars emerge like distant sighs,
Cradled in the velvet night,
A tranquil glow, the sky complies,
Guiding dreams with gentle light.

Whispers of the cosmos tease,
As constellations start to wink,
In this peace, the mind finds ease,
Lost in thoughts, we hardly think.

Softly shines the moon's embrace,
Bathing earth in silver streams,
In its calm, we find our place,
Floating freely in our dreams.

Time feels slow beneath the stars,
Each moment savored, fully grown,
Healing hearts, erasing scars,
In the dark, we are not alone.

Underneath the tranquil glow,
Hope finds roots in shimmering beams,
In the night, serenity flows,
Guiding us to brighter dreams.

# Ethereal Silence of Midnight

Midnight falls, the world asleep,
In shadows deep, the stillness breathes,
Secrets kept in silence steep,
Whispers dance between the leaves.

The stars above, like watchful eyes,
Reflecting dreams of days gone by,
In this calm, no need for sighs,
Quiet moments lift us high.

The moonlight spills a silver thread,
Tying hearts to night's embrace,
In the silence, words are said,
Painting peace upon our face.

Thoughts become like rippling streams,
Flowing softly, pure and clear,
In the quiet, hearts can dream,
Finding truths that draw us near.

Ethereal night, a soothing balm,
Wash away the cares of day,
In the still, we find our calm,
Veiling fears that drift away.

# A Celestial Riddle Unspoken

In the cosmos vast and deep,
Galaxies twirl in silent art,
A riddle woven, secrets creep,
Love and wonder play their part.

Nebulas swirl in vibrant hues,
Painting tales beyond our gaze,
In the depths, the heart imbues,
Yearning for the astral maze.

Comets blaze with fiery trails,
Carrying wishes through the night,
Echoing the ancient tales,
Of dreams danced in starlit sight.

Planets spin in timeless flight,
Structures built by cosmic hands,
In this realm of pure delight,
Awakening the heart that stands.

Unfurling mysteries abound,
In the silence of the skies,
A celestial riddle unbound,
Inviting every soul to rise.

# Tender Veil of Night

A blanket drapes the sky so deep,
Stars awaken from their sleep.
Moonlight dances on the trees,
Caressing softly in the breeze.

Shadows whisper, secrets shared,
In this quiet, hearts are bared.
Dreams take flight on silver beams,
Painting night with gentle dreams.

The world slows down, serene and still,
As dusk unfolds its tender will.
Each breath a moment, softly spun,
A symphony when day is done.

Crickets sing their lullaby,
While fireflies twinkle, drawing nigh.
Wrapped in shadows, love ignites,
Within the tender veil of night.

Close your eyes and drift away,
To where the stars forever play.
In this embrace, let worries cease,
And find your solace, find your peace.

# Whispers of the Celestial Night

In the stillness, stars align,
Whispers woven, pure divine.
Galaxies shimmer in their grace,
As dreams unfold in this vast space.

The universe breathes, alive,
Echoes of fate, we all strive.
Celestial bodies spinning round,
In their dance, our hopes are found.

Night unveils her velvet shroud,
Making mysteries feel so proud.
With every twinkle, stories told,
Of lovers lost and hearts so bold.

The moon, a guardian, glowing bright,
Guarding secrets throughout the night.
With each phase, tales are spun,
In the whispers 'neath the sun.

So listen close, let silence reign,
In the stillness, there's no pain.
Embrace the magic, feel the light,
In the whispers of the celestial night.

# In the Quiet of the Cosmic Veil

In the hush, the cosmos breathes,
Drifting whispers in the leaves.
Time stands still, our worries fade,
In the quiet, dreams are laid.

Nebulas weave their colorful threads,
In silent tales, where hope treads.
Stars connect in patterns rare,
Crafting wishes, light as air.

Infinite peace in every sigh,
Across the vast, expansive sky.
Moments linger, drifting slow,
In the cosmic veil, we flow.

The universe listens, holds us tight,
Cradling hearts through the night.
With every breath, a promise made,
In this quiet, love won't fade.

So cast your dreams into the night,
And watch them take their graceful flight.
In the quiet, the stars unveil,
A journey boundless, through the veil.

# Echoes of a Hidden Luminary

A flicker dims, then glows again,
Echoes dance in night's refrain.
A hidden light, so soft and shy,
Watches over from the sky.

In shadows cast by moonbeams bright,
Secrets shared in gentle light.
Each glimmer tells a story new,
Of distant worlds we never knew.

The starlit path, a guide so true,
Where hopes and dreams begin to brew.
In silent whispers, hearts will yearn,
For echoes of light, we'll always learn.

Alive within the cosmic play,
The luminary lights our way.
Through twists and turns, we seek to find,
The hidden spark that binds our kind.

So reach for stars, let spirits soar,
In the echoes, forevermore.
With every flicker, we embrace,
The hidden luminary's grace.

## Shy Beacons of the Night

In silken folds of velvet skies,
Stars blink softly, shy surprise.
Guiding dreams with gentle light,
Whispers echo, sheer delight.

Moonlit paths where shadows blend,
Flickers dance, the night commend.
In the stillness, secrets flow,
Shy beacons watch, their soft glow.

Underneath the quiet haze,
Wishes float in twilight's gaze.
Each beam tells a tale untold,
In the dark, their hearts unfold.

Crickets sing a lullaby,
To the hush of breezes sigh.
Together in the soft embrace,
Shy beacons light the endless space.

With every twinkle, stories meld,
In the night, our dreams are held.
Though they hide, they still ignite,
Hopeful sparks – shy beacons bright.

# Quietude in the Cosmos

In the vastness where silence reigns,
A cosmic dance, a gentle strain.
Stars in slumber softly hum,
Songs of worlds yet to become.

Galaxies in silent spin,
Whispers of where dreams begin.
Nebulae, like paintings glide,
In the quiet, all abide.

Time slows down in starlit grace,
Each heartbeat finds its rightful place.
Celestial calm enfolds the night,
In quietude, we feel the light.

Winds of wonder, softly blow,
Across the void, where secrets grow.
Among the stars, a peace so grand,
In the cosmos, hand in hand.

Breathe the stillness, let it seep,
Into your soul, where dreams can leap.
In this hush, we start to see,
The quietude that sets us free.

# Luminescence of the Unheard

In shadows cast, where echoes lie,
Secrets bloom, and whispers sigh.
The unheard speak in silent gleams,
Guided softly by our dreams.

Light that flickers, deeply felt,
Colors hidden, softly melt.
Each pulse, a story of its own,
In luminescence, we are grown.

Imagined worlds take flight and soar,
Where unseen wonders ebb and pour.
In every gleam, a heart does yearn,
For the truths we seek to learn.

Beneath the surface, magic swells,
In quiet corners, beauty dwells.
Where shadows dance, the light will play,
Luminescence brightens the way.

So listen close, to what's not said,
In every glance, in words unshed.
For in the silence, life reclaims,
The whispers of forgotten names.

## Shadows of Heavenly Glow

In twilight's hue, a canvas wide,
Shadows stretch and softly glide.
Each curve and line a gentle trace,
Of timeless beauty, calm embrace.

Stars like lanterns flicker bright,
Guiding paths through endless night.
In the dark, a story flows,
Crafted from celestial prose.

The moon casts spells, a silver hue,
Illuminating dreams anew.
Whispers linger, a soft refrain,
In shadows, we find peace again.

Through the veils of night we wander,
In silent awe we pause, we ponder.
The glow reveals what's deep inside,
In shadows, our hearts confide.

So fear not darkness, let it show,
The beauty in the heavenly glow.
Each shadow holds a light unknown,
A tapestry of night overthrown.

# Night's Gentle Radiance

In twilight's embrace, shadows play,
The moon whispers softly, guiding the way.
Stars sprinkle silver, a celestial lace,
All is serene in night's gentle grace.

Cool breezes murmur through leafy boughs,
Crickets serenade under night's vows.
The world slows down, time takes a breath,
Wrapped in the calm that dances with death.

Reflections shimmer on the quiet lake,
A mirror of dreams, a moment to take.
Each wave a secret, each ripple a tale,
Carried on currents, where night winds sail.

Eclipsed by silence, the vastness expands,
The heart listens closely to whispered commands.
In every shadow, a story resides,
Night's gentle radiance softly abides.

As dawn starts to break and pale light unfurls,
The night bids farewell, as day gently swirls.
But memories linger, never to fade,
For night's gentle radiance, forever portrayed.

# The Sigh of Starlit Sands

Beneath a canopy of twinkling light,
The sands whisper soft, in the quiet of night.
Footprints erased by the tide's gentle kiss,
Echoes of dreams found, in the abyss.

With each cautious step, the world seems to pause,
The waves tell stories, of nature's own laws.
A melody lingers where shadows extend,
The sigh of starlit sands, a wonder to send.

Moonbeams cascade on the ocean's embrace,
Painting soft silver on the water's face.
Each grain of sand holds a distant star,
A memory of light, though we are afar.

Whispers of winds weave through the night air,
Caressing the dunes, a delicate care.
The sky leans low, the horizon so wide,
The sigh of starlit sands, where secrets reside.

As morning draws near, the starlight will flee,
Yet its warmth lingers, steadfast and free.
For the sigh of starlit sands shall remain,
A timeless reminder, in joy and in pain.

# Sublime Echoes above

In the stillness above, the heavens unfold,
A tapestry woven, of stories untold.
Galaxies twinkle with pure, radiant light,
Whispers of ages in the canvas of night.

Comets that streak, like dreams on the run,
In the vastness of space, where time has begun.
Each star a whisper, a stunning refrain,
Sublime echoes above, in joy and in pain.

Nebulas blossom with colors so bright,
A dance through the cosmos, a beautiful sight.
Starlight reflects on the oceans below,
In perfect harmony, as breezes softly flow.

The cosmos a symphony, bold and profound,
Notes painted with stardust, in silence resound.
With every heartbeat, the universe sighs,
In the sublime echoes above, where hope never dies.

So gaze at the night, let the wonder ignite,
For the stars are your dreams, taking flight.
Each whisper a promise, forever shall be,
In sublime echoes above, you're truly free.

# A Secret Dance of Light

When shadows gather, and daylight withdraws,
A secret dance of light begins with applause.
Fireflies flicker in the velvet night sky,
Each glow a heartbeat, as moments pass by.

With every swirl, the stars seem to sway,
Guiding the dreams that gently decay.
The moon spins softly in its silver gown,
Whispering secrets, as the world settles down.

Each beam that breaks through the darkness around,
Illuminates whispers that dance without sound.
A tapestry woven of shadows and glow,
The secret dance of light, a mystical show.

In the hush of the night, the world holds its breath,
As fireflies weave tales of life and of death.
With every flicker, old stories relight,
In harmony soft, they embrace the night.

As dawn tiptoes in with its brushed golden hue,
The dance starts to fade, as moments turn new.
But memories linger in remnants of bright,
For in every heartbeat, lives a secret light.

# Shimmering in Silence

In the hush of the night, we find,
Stars whisper secrets, intertwined.
The moonlight dances on gentle streams,
Cradling softly our hidden dreams.

A flicker of hope in shadows cast,
Moments like echoes, forever last.
The world stands still, in quiet grace,
Time wraps us in a warm embrace.

Beneath the canopy, hearts ignite,
Fleeting visions take silent flight.
Daring to dream in the velvet dark,
Filling the air with a bright spark.

Ears attuned to the cosmos' song,
In this realm, we truly belong.
Shimmering softly, like glimmers bright,
Guiding our souls through the night.

Together we linger, hand in hand,
Creating magic in this sweet land.
In silence enchanting, we remain,
Shimmering coursing through joy and pain.

# Ethereal Glow

Glimmers adorn the dusky sky,
Like fleeting thoughts that pass us by.
A dance of colors, gentle and pure,
Whispers of dreams that always endure.

The twilight paints a canvas wide,
With every hue, time cannot hide.
A symphony sung by the stars above,
Cradling the world in waves of love.

Breathless, we watch as moments unfold,
Stories of wisdom, softly told.
Each flicker a promise, a tale untold,
In the spaces where hearts are bold.

Ethereal glow, a soft embrace,
Leading us to that sacred place.
Navigating shadows, we find the light,
As night bows down to morning's sight.

Together we wander, forever entwined,
In dreams where our spirits are aligned.
Each glowing ember, a spark of fate,
In this cosmic dance, we celebrate.

# Softly Written in the Sky

Clouds drift by in a gentle race,
Carving stories in wide-open space.
Each whisper of wind tells tales anew,
Softly written in every hue.

Across the canvas of twilight's grace,
Scribbled secrets, our hearts embrace.
The sun dips low, a golden ink,
Painting the world with twilight's wink.

Fleeting moments like softest sigh,
Brushstrokes that linger, never die.
In every gleam, a chance to soar,
Opening wide and inviting more.

Together we chase the fading light,
Where dreams are born, and joy takes flight.
Under the stars, our hopes we write,
Softly scripted in the night.

With every sunset, new tales we weave,
In this vast sky, we still believe.
In the silence, our hearts will cry,
Softly written, as night drifts by.

## The Ghost of a Glimmer

Fading echoes of a shining past,
Whispers of light that didn't last.
In the corners where shadows creep,
The ghost of a glimmer, a secret to keep.

A flicker of hope in twilight's sigh,
Remembering moments that linger nigh.
Grains of stardust drift through time,
Chasing the echoes of a distant chime.

Every heartbeat a soft reminder,
Of dreams once bright, now a bit kinder.
Solace found in the glimmers lost,
Celebrating shadows, whatever the cost.

The night holds mysteries, deep and wide,
With every twilight, we seek to abide.
In the spectral glow, in silence profound,
The ghost of a glimmer is waiting around.

As we journey through the ebb and flow,
Embracing both light and the dark we know.
The spirit of hope will always shine,
A ghost in the heart, forever divine.

## Serene Light of Distant Realms

In the hush of evening's glow,
Stars awaken, soft and slow.
Whispers dance on gentle breeze,
Filling hearts with tranquil ease.

Time drifts through the velvet night,
Chasing dreams in silver light.
Each flicker holds a tale to tell,
Of distant worlds where spirits dwell.

Moonbeams paint the skies above,
Illuminating thoughts of love.
As shadows melt in twilight's grace,
The universe begins to trace.

Paths that lead through cosmic skies,
Where every heartbeat softly sighs.
In harmony, the starlight hums,
Uniting souls as nighttime comes.

Beneath this canopy so wide,
We find our place, our hearts abide.
In every glow, a spark ignites,
Connecting us in endless nights.

# A Luminary's Lullaby

Cradled in the moon's embrace,
Dreamers find their sacred space.
Softly whispered, a gentle tune,
Guided by the watchful moon.

Stars above, like diamonds bright,
Sing to us in the still of night.
Each note flows like a silver stream,
Sowing seeds of hope and dream.

A lullaby of cosmic grace,
Wraps the world in sweet solace.
In this moment, peace takes flight,
Beneath the tapestry of night.

Hands entwined, we share this song,
Joined together, we belong.
In harmony, our spirits rise,
Beneath the watchful starlit skies.

The night will keep our secrets safe,
While dreams, like fireflies, escape.
In every heartbeat, love will grow,
In this lullaby, we lose the woe.

# The Forgotten Celestial

Once a star in twilight's throng,
Flickered briefly, then was gone.
Its tale lost in time's embrace,
A memory, a fleeting trace.

Once it danced with radiant glow,
Illuminating paths below.
Now it whispers, low and clear,
A message meant for hearts to hear.

In the silence of the void,
Hope remains, though it's destroyed.
Fragments linger in the dark,
Waiting for that final spark.

As others shine, it's not alone,
In every heart, its light has grown.
Though forgotten, it still believes,
In the magic that one receives.

Through the ages, tales will roam,
Finding solace far from home.
In the cosmos, ever true,
The forgotten will shine anew.

# Tranquil Whisper in the Vastness

In the vastness, silence reigns,
Echoes linger around the plains.
A tranquil whisper fills the air,
Carrying dreams beyond despair.

Every star a story spun,
Threads of silver, lost but won.
In this space, the heart can soar,
Finding peace forevermore.

Galaxies in rhythmic pulse,
Release their light, a cosmic impulse.
In the fabric of the night,
Truth emerges, pure and bright.

A gentle murmur calls our name,
Igniting hope, a burning flame.
Together here, we stand as one,
Beneath the gaze of the endless sun.

With every breath, we feel the call,
Of distant worlds that rise and fall.
A tranquil whisper guides us far,
Into the heart of every star.

## The Tryst of Shadows and Stars

In the night where silence breathes,
Two figures merge beneath the trees.
Shadows dance with timid grace,
Stars above in bright embrace.

Whispers linger, soft and low,
Promises of love to grow.
Moonlight spills like silver wine,
In this moment, hearts entwine.

Glimmers fade into the mist,
A fleeting touch, a gentle kiss.
Dreams alight on whispered breath,
In the tryst, they find no death.

Time dissolves like distant air,
A secret shared, a silent prayer.
With each heartbeat, worlds collide,
In tender shadows, love won't hide.

As dawn creeps in, they must part,
Yet linger still within the heart.
Underneath a waking sky,
In shadows cast, their spirits fly.

# The Luminary's Solitude

A lone star glimmers in the night,
Casting dreams in soft twilight.
Eclipsed by dark, it softly sighs,
In its stillness, wisdom lies.

A cosmic journey, silent flight,
Chasing whispers through the light.
Each moment drifts in quiet grace,
An endless search in boundless space.

From afar, the worlds unite,
In solitude, it finds its sight.
The universe holds tales untold,
In every flicker, hot and cold.

Isolation, yet a spark,
A glowing ember in the dark.
To guide the lost in time's embrace,
A luminary's sacred space.

As night fades into dawn's warm flame,
It whispers softly, calls its name.
Though alone, it finds its way,
In solitude, it learns to stay.

## Cosmic Chill of a Whispered Dawn

As night surrenders to the light,
A chill lingers, soft and bright.
Whispers echo through the air,
Secrets shared without a care.

Stars begin to fade away,
In the glow of the new day.
The cosmos hums a gentle tune,
Breathing life with the coming moon.

Frosty tendrils brush the earth,
Marking time with quiet mirth.
Each moment holds a cosmic breath,
In the stillness, life and death.

Awakening dreams in dawn's embrace,
A soft light spills, a warming grace.
Nature stirs in chill of morn,
In whispers, new worlds are born.

Through the skies, a story weaves,
Of hopes that linger in the leaves.
From cosmic chills to the day's bright yawn,
Life unfolds with whispered dawn.

## Hushed Light of Another World

In shadows cast by silver beams,
Another world spins through dreams.
Hushed light dances on the ground,
In a silent symphony, profound.

Orbiting secrets, deep and wide,
Celestial wonders softly glide.
Mysteries held in twilight's hand,
Glimpses of a far-off land.

Galaxies hum a soothing song,
In this realm, where we belong.
A quiet peace, a heart that swells,
With the stories that time tells.

As twilight deepens, whispers start,
Rising gently, touching the heart.
Each flicker holds a tale untold,
In hushed light, the universe unfolds.

In ethereal glow, we dream of flight,
Seeking solace in the night.
With each heartbeat, worlds entwined,
In the hushed light, love is defined.

# Tryst of Light and Silence

In the quiet glow, secrets meet,
Whispers linger where shadows greet.
Stars align in a dance so bright,
Together they weave the threads of night.

Beneath the moon's watchful eye,
Dreams unfold and softly sigh.
In this moment, time stands still,
Hearts entwined, they drink their fill.

Glimmers fade as dawn draws near,
Yet the echo remains, crystal clear.
In the twilight's tender embrace,
Light and silence, a sacred space.

Though day may chase the night away,
Memories linger in soft array.
In the heart's cradle, they softly dwell,
The tryst of light, the tale they tell.

Each dawn heralds a fleeting chance,
To find the magic in life's expanse.
For in silence, the truth does ignite,
A union forged in purest light.

## Celestial Hush

In the stillness of the night sky,
Stars whisper secrets, oh so shy.
Galaxies swirl in a cosmic dance,
Wrapped in a shimmering trance.

A hush blankets the world below,
As the universe begins to glow.
Celestial wonders, vast and bright,
Guide wanderers seeking the light.

Timeless tales in stardust spun,
Each twinkle a story, a journey begun.
Dreamers gaze, with hearts full of hope,
In the cosmos, they learn to cope.

Between the stars, silence sings,
Carrying the weight of countless things.
In this darkness, clarity shines,
The secrets of existence entwined.

Yet as dawn breaks the spell of night,
The cosmos whispers in fading light.
In the heart, the silence remains,
Celestial whispers echo in veins.

# The Solitary Spark

In the depths of the night, a spark ignites,
Lonely flickers dance with the heights.
A beacon of hope in shadows deep,
Guarding dreams that softly seep.

Amidst the void, a gentle glow,
Casting warmth on the world below.
Though solitary, it stands so bright,
Defying the darkness with sheer light.

Time may dim the brightest flame,
Yet the spark remains, unashamed.
For in the silence, it finds its way,
Through the depths of night to the break of day.

Resilient and fierce, it holds its ground,
A testament to strength profound.
In solitude, there lies great power,
A solitary spark in the darkest hour.

As dawn approaches, shadows flee,
The spark endures, wild and free.
In the journey of life, a truth is found,
Even alone, love can abound.

# Beyond the Shimmering Veil

Through the mist, a whisper calls,
Promising wonders beyond the walls.
A shimmering veil, soft and light,
Guides the lost through the endless night.

Veils of fate, elusive and grand,
Hold the stories of the unseen land.
With each step, the heart takes flight,
Chasing dreams into the light.

Beyond horizons, the spirit dances,
In the glow of uncounted chances.
Mysteries unfold like petals in bloom,
Inviting all to escape the gloom.

Yet, as dawn breaks through the haze,
The veil dissolves, revealing a maze.
Paths diverge and stories entwine,
In the journey, the stars align.

So venture forth with open heart,
Embrace the world, play your part.
For beyond the veil, a tapestry weaves,
The essence of life in what one believes.

# The Gentle Dusk of Luminous Dreams

As daylight fades to tender hues,
Soft whispers call from twilight's muse.
Stars awaken in the velvet sky,
While shadows dance as night draws nigh.

In golden glimmers, wishes fly,
Woven in the air, they sigh.
The moon, a guardian high above,
Casts silver beams like gentle love.

Each heartbeat echoes dreams anew,
In the dusk's embrace, they brew.
Tender thoughts in silence scheme,
Painted softly, the night redeem.

The world now breathes a softer sound,
In hushed tones, where peace is found.
Dusk cradles all in its warm fold,
And stories of old begin to unfold.

So let us wander, hand in hand,
Through dusky paths of wonderland.
Embrace the night, let worries cease,
In luminous dreams, we find our peace.

# Shimmering in Solitude

In quiet corners where thoughts reside,
Solitude glimmers, a tranquil tide.
Each moment breathes a lighter air,
As shadows fade and hearts lay bare.

The gentle rustle of the leaves,
Whispers secrets the silence weaves.
Stars wink softly, a distant glance,
Inviting souls to join the dance.

Alone yet full, the spirit sings,
With every note, the heart takes wings.
In shadows deep, reflections gleam,
In solitude's embrace, we dream.

The world outside may rush and roar,
But here, within, there lies so much more.
In this still space, I find my light,
Shimmering gently through the night.

And as I linger, time stands still,
Wrapped in the quiet, I drink my fill.
In solitude's dance, I claim my part,
A shimmering echo, a sacred heart.

# A Lullaby from Distant Realms

A lullaby drifts from worlds unknown,
Carried on breezes soft and lone.
Tales of starlight in whispers dance,
Inviting the dreamers to take a chance.

In twilight's embrace, where shadows sway,
Melodies bloom in a gentle play.
In the silence, secrets unfold,
Cradling dreams in stories told.

With every note, the heart takes flight,
Crossing the borders of day and night.
From distant realms, the echoes call,
Softly weaving through the hall.

As moonlight drapes the earth like lace,
In this lullaby, I find my place.
With every sigh and every breath,
I dance with shadows and flirt with death.

So let the song wrap round my soul,
As I surrender to its control.
From distant realms, I'll find my way,
In lullabies that softly sway.

# Ethereal Glow of Unheard Melodies

In the silence, music softly glows,
Ethereal whispers where the stardust flows.
Notes unspoken, hidden from sight,
Drifting gently on the edge of night.

Each heartbeat echoes the melody near,
In the stillness, a symphony clear.
Shadows move to an unheard tune,
Dancing beneath the watchful moon.

In twilight's arms, the magic starts,
Binding souls, weaving their arts.
Every glance, a note, every sigh,
In this silent concert, we learn to fly.

Though no voice brings forth the song,
In each moment, we find we belong.
With ethereal glow, our spirits rise,
Caught in the music beneath the skies.

And as we journey through this night,
In unheard melodies, we find our light.
Together we'll wander, hearts set free,
In the ethereal glow, just you and me.

# Beneath the Veil of Twinkling Dreams

In night's embrace, stars softly sigh,
Whispers of hopes drift through the sky.
Gentle shadows dance, bathed in light,
While dreams take flight, hidden from sight.

A canvas rich with silver and blue,
Secrets of hearts, old and anew.
Under the veil, wishes unfold,
Stories of love in silence retold.

Paths of stardust call us near,
Echoes of laughter blend with the sphere.
Ethereal glow on the world below,
Beneath twinkling dreams, where fantasies flow.

Each shimmer a heartbeat, each flash a prayer,
Infinite beauty floating in air.
Beneath luminous skies, we wander free,
In the grasp of visions, endlessly.

Night's lullaby wraps us in its grace,
Time transcends in this sacred space.
Beneath the veil, our spirits soar high,
Together we dance, you and I.

## Solitude in the Celestial Sea

Under the vastness, alone I drift,
Waves of silence, a haunting gift.
Stars above like mirrors reflect,
The solitude, tender yet direct.

The moon whispers secrets in twilight's embrace,
Lost in the rhythm of time and space.
Each star a companion, yet worlds apart,
In cosmic solitude, I find my heart.

Gentle tides pull at the edges of dreams,
Where echoes linger, and stillness schemes.
Floating amid the shimmering light,
Embraced by shadows, I welcome the night.

Celestial wonders twinkle above,
In the expanse of the void, I feel love.
A universe bustling, yet still I stay,
In my own solitude, I find my way.

With each heartbeat, the stars align,
Connecting moments, both yours and mine.
In this celestial sea, so vast, so bright,
I sail through the darkness, into the light.

## The Forgotten Luminescence

Time has hushed the city's cry,
As daylight fades beneath the sky.
Lost memories flicker, gentle and sweet,
In shadows where old worlds meet.

Once vibrant colors now dim and pale,
Whispers of stories drift in the veil.
Flickers of warmth from moments gone,
The heart remembers, though light has withdrawn.

In corners where laughter used to live,
Echoes of joy, the past still gives.
Luminescence forgotten, yet ever near,
A gentle reminder that we once were here.

Through the darkness, small sparks arise,
Igniting the night with their silent cries.
Threads of existence weave through the haze,
A dance of remembrance, a flickering blaze.

The world may forget the light we share,
Yet in each heartbeat, the glow's aware.
From shadows we rise, our essence set free,
In the forgotten, we find our decree.

# Dreaming of Distant Radiance

In a world of echoes, my thoughts take flight,
Chasing the glow of a distant light.
Beyond the horizons, where wishes reside,
In dreams, my heart opens wide.

Radiance beckons from far-off domains,
Drawing me close through the soft, gentle rains.
Each droplet whispers tales of the bright,
Of realms untouched by the depth of night.

Imagined landscapes painted in gold,
Adventures await, stories untold.
Together we traverse the cosmic expanse,
In dreams of radiance, we find our chance.

The tapestry woven with threads of our hope,
Guides us through shadows where we learn to cope.
With each dazzling glimmer, we rise and proclaim,
That dreams are the keys to the fortune we claim.

So let us wander through spaces untamed,
Where every heartbeat ignites a new flame.
Distant radiance shimmers, endlessly clear,
In the realm of dreams, I hold you near.

# Whispers in the Milky Way

Stars twinkle softly, secrets untold,
Galaxies dance in the vastness of cold.
Whispers of starlight, sweet and serene,
Galactic murmurs wrap the unseen.

Nebulas bloom in colors so bright,
Echoes of wonders lost in the night.
Each flicker is hope, a guiding spark,
Lost souls find solace in the dark.

Through cosmic threads, we seek and we roam,
In the expanse, we find our true home.
Celestial melodies forming a tune,
Each note caressing the light of the moon.

With every heartbeat, the universe sighs,
In the silence, our spirit flies high.
Dreaming of worlds beyond what we see,
In the Milky Way, we are truly free.

Together we wander, hand in hand,
Through starlit paths, where dreams expand.
Each whisper a promise, a tale to unfold,
In the arms of the cosmos, our stories told.

# A Dream of Distant Gleams

On the horizon, horizons of gold,
Waves of starlight, mysteries unfold.
Comets trailing secrets from afar,
Guided by visions of each distant star.

A symphony hums in the quiet of night,
Echoing softly, a shimmering light.
In the expanse, dreams take their flight,
Painting the cosmos in colors so bright.

Timeless whispers through celestial streams,
Beacons of hope, igniting our dreams.
With every twinkle, the promise of fate,
In the celestial dance, we cultivate.

Gazing upward, hearts open wide,
Cradled gently by the cosmic tide.
Each moment a treasure, a glimpse of the grand,
A dream of distant gleams, hand in hand.

With stardust courage, we dare to believe,
In the magic of night, we weave and achieve.
In the tapestry vast, where all stories align,
A dream of distant gleams forever will shine.

## Unseen Guidance

In shadows of twilight, whispers arise,
Unseen guidance beneath starlit skies.
A touch of the cosmos, gentle yet clear,
Leading the way, dissolving our fear.

Stars align softly, a dance of the fate,
Each glimmer a pulse, a silent debate.
Echoes of wisdom in the lunar glow,
Guiding our journey, where we must go.

Through darkness and doubt, a beacon is found,
Carried by hope, unbroken, profound.
In moments of silence, we hear the call,
Unseen guidance supports us through all.

With every heartbeat, a promise is sealed,
In vastness of night, our wounds are revealed.
Connected by souls from realms yet untold,
The universe whispers, steadfast and bold.

Together we walk, side by side,
In the arms of the stars, we take our stride.
Each step a reminder, love's gentle embrace,
Unseen guidance surrounds us through space.

# Glimmering Heartbeats of Infinity

In the silent expanse, hearts resonate,
Glimmering pulses, an eternal state.
Through the void, our spirits entwine,
In heartbeats of stardust, we shine.

Galaxies swirl in a breathtaking dance,
Inviting our souls to take a chance.
In love's soft embrace, we rise and we fall,
Glimmering heartbeats connect us all.

Whispers of memories, echoes of time,
In the grand tapestry, we find our rhyme.
Each flicker a promise, a bond that won't break,
With every heartbeat, new paths we make.

In shadows of night, we safely reside,
Glimmering heartbeats, our love as our guide.
Through the cosmos together, we sail,
Infinity's embrace, we shall never fail.

As stars guide our way, we forever align,
In the dance of existence, our souls intertwine.
Through every moment, the universe sings,
Glimmering heartbeats of infinite things.

# Twilight's Secret

In the hush of the evening glow,
Shadows dance as soft winds blow.
Whispers hide in the fading light,
Stars emerge, twinkling bright.

Secrets linger, time stands still,
Hearts awaken to the thrill.
Colors blend, a canvas rare,
Night's embrace, a tender care.

Beneath the sky, dreams take flight,
Lost in wonder, pure delight.
In the twilight's warm embrace,
We find solace, a sacred space.

As horizons melt into night,
We chase echoes of lost light.
A realm where day meets the dark,
Igniting hope with a spark.

In the silence, stories weave,
Tales of love that we believe.
Embracing dreams, we softly tread,
Twilight's secret, softly said.

# Embracing the Unseen Luminary

In the depths of a quiet heart,
Lies a glow, a sacred part.
Unseen light that guides our way,
A luminary in the gray.

With every breath, we draw it near,
Trusting whispers, calm and clear.
In the chaos, stillness reigns,
Embracing joy, releasing pains.

Invisible threads, softly spun,
Connecting all, we are as one.
In unity, we find the spark,
Illuminating paths so stark.

Each dream we nurture, gently grow,
Revealing truths we long to know.
Guided by a light unseen,
In the dark, we find the serene.

Together, we create and weave,
A tapestry of what we believe.
In shadows cast, our spirits soar,
Embracing love forevermore.

# The Stillness Beyond

In the quiet, a gentle sigh,
Where time pauses, moments lie.
Whispers echo through the air,
In stillness, find a sacred care.

Mountains watch, the rivers flow,
Nature sings in quiet glow.
In the heart of silence, peace,
From the chaos, sweet release.

Beneath the stars, dreams are spun,
In the night sky, we become one.
Eternal secrets softly dwell,
In the stillness, all is well.

The night breathes deep, a calming balm,
Resting here, we feel the calm.
With every heartbeat, we align,
In unity, our souls entwine.

In echoes vast, we find our song,
In this silence, we belong.
Each moment cherished, time expands,
The stillness beyond, as love demands.

## Starry Dreams Unspoken

Under blankets of night unfurled,
Lost in dreams of another world.
Stars above, like eyes that gleam,
Whispering softly, a shared dream.

In the silence, secrets dwell,
Woven stories we cannot tell.
Each twinkle, a wish cast high,
A fleeting thought, as time drifts by.

Magic in the midnight air,
Yearning hearts, a silent prayer.
In the stillness, we reach out,
Starry dreams, of hope and doubt.

With every breath, a wish unfolds,
In layers of light, our fate molds.
Holding tight to moments rare,
In the vastness, we declare.

Every star, a path we trace,
Guiding us through time and space.
In their glow, we find our voice,
Starry dreams, we rejoice.

# Flickers of Tranquil Eternity

In the stillness of dawn's first light,
Dreams awaken, soft and bright.
Whispers dance on the breeze,
Time slows down, hearts at ease.

Petals open to the sun's embrace,
Nature beckons, a gentle grace.
Moments linger, calm and clear,
Fleeting joys draw us near.

Beneath the stars, the river flows,
Singing secrets only it knows.
Reflecting skies of endless hue,
In tranquil depths, we find what's true.

With every wave, a story shared,
In the stillness, souls laid bare.
Embracing silence, we find peace,
A flicker of time that will not cease.

Here in the quiet, we remain,
Boundless love amidst the rain.
Eternity's breath, soft and slow,
In the heart's cradle, we let go.

# The Cosmic Hush of Yesteryears

In the twilight, shadows blend,
Whispers of time, they never end.
Stars recount old tales untold,
Fading memories, glimmers of gold.

Through the cosmos, echoes resound,
Every heartbeat, ancient ground.
Connections deep within our soul,
In silence, we find the whole.

Moments drift like clouds on high,
Painting memories in the sky.
The universe holds each refrain,
With cosmic hush, we break the chain.

Threads of time softly entwine,
In the fabric, we seek the line.
The past whispers through every star,
Guiding us back to who we are.

In the stillness, history glows,
A celestial path that gently flows.
Yesteryears dance in quiet grace,
With the cosmos, we find our place.

# Echoing Light of Solitary Nights

Underneath the veil of night,
Stars cast down their shards of light.
Lonely paths stretch far and wide,
In the dark, hope can abide.

Moonbeams tracing lost designs,
Sending forth their silver signs.
Whispers echo, soft as air,
In the stillness, hearts laid bare.

Into shadows, dreams take flight,
Guided by the gentle night.
Each flicker tells a silent tale,
Of wanderers who set their sails.

Solitude, a solemn friend,
In its grasp, we start to mend.
Echoes linger, a soft embrace,
In the dark, we find our place.

With every glance at the starlit sky,
Hope awakens, even when shy.
Echoing light, a sacred part,
In solitary nights, we find heart.

# Radiance Without a Voice

In the silence, colors bloom,
Echoing light dispels the gloom.
Beauty breathes without a sound,
In its warmth, our hearts are found.

Golden rays touch every face,
Radiance weaves a gentle grace.
Moments stitched in vibrant hue,
Speaking truths that feel so new.

A dance of shadows, flickers bright,
Illuminating wings of night.
Each heartbeat resonates with light,
In the stillness, we take flight.

Colors whisper softly here,
In their presence, love draws near.
Radiance flows, a sacred stream,
Guiding souls to share the dream.

Voices silent, yet so clear,
In the glow, we conquer fear.
Through every shade, we find our choice,
Embracing life in radiance, no voice.

# Lost in the Cradle of Infinity

In the void where dreams entwine,
Stars whisper secrets so divine.
Galaxies swirl, a dance of time,
Echoes of light in cosmic rhyme.

Celestial sails on endless seas,
Cradled gently by cosmic breezes.
Infinite thoughts drift like a breeze,
Awakening wonders, hearts at ease.

In silence, the universe sings clear,
Each twinkle a wish, each breath a tear.
Lost in the cradle, we find our way,
Boundless horizons beckon to stay.

Through the dark, a beacon glows,
Guiding the lost where the river flows.
An odyssey bright in shadows gray,
Hopeful souls seeking a vibrant ray.

In the heart of space, we softly drift,
Among the stars, our spirits lift.
Embraced by the night, we come alive,
In the cradle of infinity, we thrive.

# The Unseen Glow of Oblivion

In shadows deep, where whispers dwell,
The unseen glow casts a quiet spell.
Past the edges of time's fading thread,
Lies a place where lost dreams are led.

Veils of light through the silence flow,
Painting the paths where the lost souls go.
Oblivion's grace, a soft embrace,
In the darkness, we find our place.

Mysteries woven in cosmic thread,
Echoes of laughter, whispers of dread.
In the unseen glow, secrets unfold,
Stories of futures, both new and old.

Through tangled tales of forgotten lore,
We wander the realms, forevermore.
Every heartbeat a pulsing star,
Illuminating dreams from afar.

In the silence, we hear the call,
Of forgotten memories, one and all.
The invisible light, a guiding force,
Leading us home on an endless course.

Together still in twilight's embrace,
Finding solace in time and space.
The unseen glow, our gentle guide,
In oblivion's arms, we will abide.

## Serenity Among the Astral Winds

Beneath the night, a tranquil sea,
Stars above hum a melody.
Among the winds that softly play,
Serenity calls us to stay.

Galactic dreams drift on the air,
Whispers of hope, a cosmic prayer.
In the stillness, our spirits soar,
Touching the heavens, craving more.

Celestial tides pull us near,
From distant worlds, their voices clear.
Among the lights, we find our truth,
In the calm, we renew our youth.

Peaceful horizons stretch, unfold,
Tales of wonder waiting to be told.
In the dance of stars, we find our blend,
Harmony's song, our perfect mend.

As astral winds in silence glide,
We chase the dreams that softly hide.
In each soft breath, the cosmos hums,
Serenity breathes, as stillness comes.

Together we drift, in starlit streams,
Wrapped in the fabric of fragile dreams.
Among the astral winds, we roam,
In tranquility's arms, we call it home.

# The Quietude of Stellar Hope

In the stillness of the cosmic night,
Lies a hope that burns so bright.
Stars twinkle softly, casting dreams,
In the darkness, a light that beams.

Quietude reigns where shadows play,
Filling the void with gentle sway.
In the silence, we find our way,
Guided by starlight's warm display.

Each pulse of light, a promise tells,
Of worlds beyond where magic dwells.
In tranquility's hold, hearts entwine,
Beneath the canopy of designs.

Hope dances in the midnight air,
Carried by dreams, free from despair.
In the cosmic sea, love's embrace,
Flourishing bright in this timeless space.

With every heartbeat, the universe calls,
Inviting the dreamers, the lovers, the thralls.
In the quietude of a starlit glow,
We find the strength to rise, to grow.

Together we soar on wings of night,
In the boundless quest for radiant light.
The quietude sings of hope so clear,
In every heartbeat, the cosmos near.

# The Peaceful Beacon

In the quiet of night, it stands bright,
Guiding lost souls with its gentle light.
A calm in the chaos, a shimmer of grace,
A steadfast reminder in this vast space.

Across the waters, its rays softly dance,
Inviting the weary, offering a chance.
Hope is ignited with each gleam it shows,
A promise of shelter from life's heavy woes.

Through storms and the shadows, it shines ever clear,
Calling the wanderers, soothing their fear.
As echoes of silence envelop the night,
The beacon's warm glow remains a pure sight.

Bringing together the hearts once apart,
It whispers of courage, igniting the heart.
With each passing moment, it steadily beams,
Lighting the pathways of forgotten dreams.

In the dawn, it fades, yet still holds its place,
A glow in our spirits, a tranquil embrace.
Forever a symbol of hope and of peace,
The beacon will shine, and our worries will cease.

## Covert Illuminations

In the silence of shadows, secrets unfold,
Unseen yet present, a story retold.
Flickering softly, in corners so small,
These covert illuminations enchant us all.

A glint of the moonlight upon empty streets,
Whispers of laughter, where mystery meets.
Hidden reflections that dance in the night,
A tapestry woven with threads of soft light.

Beneath the still surface of tranquil lakes,
Glories of starlight, small ripples it makes.
In fleeting glimpses, we catch our own fate,
These fleeting impressions, a mirage innate.

Secrets and shadows entwined in the air,
A flicker of hope found in moments so rare.
In darkened corners, where dreams come alive,
Covert illuminations, for hearts that strive.

As dawn approaches, the magic subsides,
Yet within our memories, the wonder abides.
For even in daylight, its essence remains,
Covert illuminations where mystery reigns.

# The Forgotten Light

In the attic of dreams, a lamp sits alone,
Whispers of days when it brightly shone.
Dust gathers slowly, covering the past,
Memories linger, refusing to last.

Faded and worn, its glow sealed in time,
A beacon of laughter, now lost to the grime.
Yet in its silence, a promise will stay,
The forgotten light hopes to find its way.

Once it danced joyously in children's delight,
Casting playful shadows through long summer nights.
With stories it told, and dreams it inspired,
The forgotten light, still quietly admired.

Unseen by the world in the hurried race,
It waits for a moment to rekindle its grace.
Awakened by memories, our hearts ignite,
As we blow off the dust and revive the light.

For even in darkness, its echoes can sing,
Reminding the weary of the hope they can bring.
The forgotten light, though dimmed, is not gone,
A flicker in shadows, always lives on.

# Hushed Glimmers in the Dark

In the cloak of the night, soft glimmers appear,
Whispers of light that the dark holds dear.
Stars like secrets, scattered and bright,
Hushed glimmers emerge, bathing all in their light.

A shimmer on water, a twinkle in trees,
Nature's own canvas, painted with ease.
Each flicker a story, a heartbeat, a spark,
These hushed glimmers whisper, even in dark.

The glow of a firefly, a lantern's embrace,
Invisible pathways, we slowly retrace.
In quiet moments, when shadows are cast,
Hushed glimmers remind us of the joys of the past.

As dreams take their flight on the wings of the night,
Each twinkling star offers poetic insight.
Tender reflections of hope shining through,
Hushed glimmers in darkness, each one is for you.

So let the night wrap you in its soft weave,
Embrace the quiet, the magic, believe.
For in every dark corner, there's beauty to find,
Hushed glimmers in darkness, brilliantly kind.

Milton Keynes UK
Ingram Content Group UK Ltd.
UKHW010228111224
452348UK00011B/583